Looking Out From Death

Duoduo

Looking Out
From Death

from the
Cultural Revolution
to Tiananmen Square

the new
Chinese poetry
of Duoduo

translated by
Gregory Lee
and
John Cayley

BLOOMSBURY

Calligraphy on the title page is by Joseph S. P. Lo, Paolin Chinese Language Services.

First published in Great Britain 1989

Bloomsbury Publishing Ltd
2 Soho Square
London W1V 5DE

ISBN 0 7475 0555 1

A CIP catalogue record for this book is available from the British Library.

Text designed and typeset by Wellsweep
Printed by Richard Clay, Bungay, Suffolk

*this book is dedicated
to all those
struggling for a voice
in China today
and to those who have died
in that struggle*

Contents

Translations marked *(JC)* are by John Cayley.
All others are by Gregory Lee.

INTRODUCTION

Duoduo, whose original name is Li Shizheng, was born in Peking in 1951. He started writing poetry in the early 1970s during the dark days of the Cultural Revolution, which lasted until 1976.* Duoduo has always been something of a maverick and an extrovert. Now working as a journalist on a national newspaper, he once trained as an opera singer and has also tried his hand at painting.

Duoduo's poetry, like that of many of his contemporaries, lies in the modernist vein, the antithesis of the officially favoured realism of the communist Chinese literary establishment. Although he is one of a number of younger poets who have achieved a reputation over the last ten years, his work is unique. His poetry has, moreover, received that hard-won accolade — the admiration of his fellow poets. He is, in effect, a poet's poet.

Unlike a number of other contemporary writers, Duoduo has not been outspoken on social or political issues, which is perhaps one reason why his reputation has taken longer to become established. Nevertheless, his gradually maturing, innately talented poetry has acquired a dedicated, sophisticated readership. He has been widely published in both the official and unofficial press (depending on the political climate) and he has given poetry readings on numerous occasions, notably at Peking University.

While Duoduo is a thoroughly Chinese poet, and shows little sign of the derivative and banal pastiche that mars the work of many contemporary Chinese poets, he is a thoroughly modern poet whose work demonstrates selective and cosmopolitan influences. He is a keen admirer of Robert Desnos, Dylan Thomas, Sylvia Plath, Marina Tsvetaeva — one of the poems in this volume is written in homage to her — and the father of modernism, Baudelaire.

In Duoduo's work we find one of the most refreshing, recent manifestations of Chinese modernism. Other poets, earlier in the century, had already started down the road of modernist

---

* Li Shizheng took the penname 'Duoduo' from the given name of a daughter who died in infancy. Its approximate pronunciation is 'Door-door' and is sometimes written 'Duo Duo'.

experimentation, but for both political and historical reasons, their attempts were short-lived. Now Duoduo's development through the 1970s and 1980s has provided China with an accomplished modernist poet, who promises to produce ever more innovative and startling poetry, imbued with genuine and intense personal feeling. His is a poetry which is at once an expressive, individual reaction to Peking life and, at the same time, a poetry which is committed to its own quest for universal truths.

As witnessed in this selection of Duoduo's verse, his poetry ranges from more openly expressed sentiments to guarded revelations of his emotions and poetic visions. Underneath his intense, passionate, but carefully controlled poetic voice, lies a barely restrained hysteria. Like Sylvia Plath's, his poetry can tremble with an awesome fear, just beneath its skin-like surface.

The fear and oppression generated by living in society — not just the awesome, turgid, suppressive society that China has been, but any society — peopled by those who seem not to understand, but who can only mock, terrorize or hunt down, is expressed in Duoduo's 'Looking out from death':

> Looking out from death you will always see
> those whom all your life you ought not to see.
> One can always be buried somewhere at one's leisure
> sniff around at one's leisure, then bury oneself there
> in a place that makes them hate.
>
> They shovel dirt in your face.
> You should thank them. And thank them again.
> For your eyes will never again see your enemy.
> Then from death will come,
> when they are consumed by enmity, a scream
> although you will never hear again:
> Now that is the absolute scream of anguish!

This is a modern, totally authentic poem, reminiscent of the classic exemplar by Baudelaire 'Le Mort Joyeux' (The Merry Dead Man) with which Duoduo's poem shares a similar theme and central image:

Dans une terre grasse et pleine d'escargots
Je veux creuser moi-même une fosse profonde,
Où je puisse à loisir étaler mes vieux os
Et dormir dans l'oubli comme un requin dans l'onde.

Je hais les testaments et je hais les tombeaux;
Plutôt que d'implorer une larme du monde,
Vivant, j'aimerais mieux inviter les corbeaux
A saigner tous les bouts de ma carcasse immonde.

[In fertile soil, full of snails,
I want to dig myself a grave,
Where I may stretch my old bones at leisure,
And sleep in oblivion like a shark in the tide.

I hate testaments and tombs,
Rather than beg the world for a tear,
Alive, I'd rather ask the crows
To bleed all the bits of my vile carcass.]

Common to both poems is the achievement of moral victory over those who would pursue the socially disaffected to self-burial. As well as their bitterness and mocking irony the two poems also share a universal theme, and yet Duoduo's poem is the product of a particular time and place, and a distinctive new voice. .

On 5th June Duoduo arrived in London for a prearranged poetry reading tour. It was to have been a time of joy, a time of exploration — it was his first time in the West. But the events he witnessed at Tiananmen Square on the eve of his departure turned his visit into a time of mourning, a time of anxiety.

As a reporter and as an ordinary citizen of Peking, Duoduo lived through the events at Tiananmen from April right up to the night and day of the 4th June massacre. That night as he ducked the bullets on Tiananmen Square, fear and repression were once more about to grip China. History was on the point of repeating itself.

Duoduo has written of this fear, which is not new to China. And in hindsight, much of his poetry may be seen as uncannily prophetic. Reading through those of his poems written in the atmosphere of terror and oppression that characterized the decade of the Cultural Revolution (1966-76), one senses that history is repeating itself, that China is now being plunged back into the same old nightmare. In interpreting this nightmare Duoduo is more than a mere poet, he is a seer.

And yet Duoduo believes the role of a poet does not lie merely in reacting against the forces of oppression, in whatever form they may be encountered, but in interpreting human relations and describing nature; themes which are not limited by time and place.

As this book goes to press, China is once more experiencing uncertainty and trauma. Whatever the eventual outcome, the fact that poets such as Duoduo can still come to the fore in China is a tribute to that country's poetic tradition, and to the universal and irrepressible poetic spirit of humanity.

Gregory Lee

On this Edition, the Original Texts and the Translations

This book is based on a small-press edition of English translations from Duoduo's work made by the Wellsweep Press. That edition was planned in late April to coincide with Duoduo's first visit to Great Britain in June 1989. Publication in the present form has made possible an extensive expansion and revision of the text in the Wellsweep book which will reach a much wider readership, and serve it better. Duoduo's close cooperation with this work and the sudden availability of his newest writing, makes the present book far more representative and authoritative.

The original Chinese texts of poems translated here can be found in a number of different Chinese collections. In rough order of their date of publication, these are as follows:

Xin Shichao Shiji (Anthology of New Wave Poetry), Lao Mu ed., Peking: Beijing Daxue Wusi Wenxue She, 1985, pages 385-435
Dangdai Zhongguo Shige Qishiwu Shou (Seventy-five Contemporary Chinese Poems), Beiling and Meng Lang eds., Peking & Shanghai: s.n., 1985
Licheng: Duoduo Shixuan: 1972-1988 (Milestones: the Selected Poems of Duoduo), [Peking], 1988 (*Shoujie Jintian Jianghuo Jiangzhe Zuopin Ji*, Winning Collection from the First 'Today' Group Poetry Prize)
Xingli: Shi 38 Shou (Greetings: 38 Poems), Duoduo zhu, Guilin: Lijiang Chubanshe, 1988 (*Qingnian Shicong. 1*; New poetry, 1)
Xingcunzhe (Survivor), Peking: Xingcunzhe Shiren Julebu, No. 1 (July 1988) and No. 2 (n.d.)

The texts used are as published, although there are many cases where differing versions of a single poem appear in one or other collection. In these cases, the translators have consulted the poet to determine the best readings. In a number of instances the translators have also taken account of unpublished corrections made later by the poet himself and discussed in the final preparation of this book.

Two of the poems in this collection are previously unpublished, here or in China. These are: *The Great Tree* and *Bell Sound*.

The order of the poems is chiefly chronological and otherwise determined by Duoduo himself. In a number of instances he has chosen to rearrange and edit earlier sequences of poems.

The translators were able to consult existing English versions for only a few poems, but would like to give particular acknowledgement to the translator of those in the small collection: Depth of Flames: poems by Duo Duo, trans Jin Zhong, Peking: s.n., 1989.

This book was produced quickly and under great pressure. Inevitably, it will contain deficiencies and errors which would have been noticed and corrected given more time, and the opportunity to consult more knowledgeable colleagues. We trust that our readers will forgive (and communicate) any infelicities they discover, while welcoming a unique, new collection of contemporary Chinese writing which might not otherwise have seen the light of day in the West. Every effort has been made to do a sound job in the time available, and Duoduo himself has actively — apart from anything else, through his unflagging, good-humoured assistance — endorsed our efforts.

Thanks are due to Isabelle Lee and Zhang Changli for their assistance and patience; and to Harriet for hers.

Looking Out From Death

the new
Chinese poetry
of Duoduo

THIS SUN OF MINE

Applause hammers at the door of May:
— hallucination — echo
— a young doctor getting to his feet in Spring:
ice melting, melting, melting....

The old father,
as he comes back to life
   — feeble with age but mighty —
as the ice flows and rolls along the river banks,
he sends up the cloud of his glory with humility.
Mother, lost deep in the birch-wood
preserves her dry, faded memories:
things past, held leaf by leaf in her book,
while younger brother is already fully-grown:
   they stretch their four limbs, breathe deep and strong....

Take a great wide brush and write: TODAY
WE ARE STILL FACING, AS ALWAYS,
STILL FACING THE FOREST KEEPERS IN THEIR GREEN
                              UNIFORMS.

1972

THOUGHTS AND RECOLLECTIONS

When the People Stand Up Out of the Hard Cheese

The sound of gunfire — dilutes the bloody terror of revolution.
August is stretched like a cruel bow.
The poisonous man-child walks out of a peasant hovel
with tobacco and a parched throat.
The cattle have been brutally blinkered
and remains hang in the hair from their haunches, like swollen
                                        clappers.
Now even the sacrifice behind the bamboo fence is obscured:
far off, the troops keep coming through the cloud.

1972

At Parting

The green fields are like constructions of the mind which have
                                              suddenly
collapsed, like an unending, boundless twilight
where the future's serried ranks keep marching on.
You, you are like someone pushed onto an unfamiliar path,
walking down a side alley, grown older
— those lights from countless family dwellings
      and one shadow of loneliness.
There is only a shepherd, tightly gripping his scarlet switch:
    — he is watching the darkness,
                  he is watching over the darkness.

1972

Blessings

When society has difficulty giving birth
that thin, black widow ties magic charms on a bamboo rod
which she waves at the rising moon.
A blood-soaked streamer emits an endless stench,
makes vicious mutts everywhere howl the whole night long.

From that superstitious time on
the motherland was led by another father,
wandering in the parks of London and the streets of Michigan,
staring with orphan's eyes at hurried steps that come and go
and again and again stuttering out old hopes and humiliations.

1973

Auspicious Day

As if it were not already over,
as if the sacrificial wine were not already finished,
outside the prison the first light of day breaks through
and the branch clumsily blossoms.
The shame of a lifetime already redeemed,
dream , although memory is still fresh, resounds like a bugle:

Wind, cannot blow away the desires of early years.
On harvested land
under the shining sun
those wretched, idle villages.
As usual thoughts revive,
as usual putting the life of freedom out to pasture ——

1973

Untitled

You are a people both swollen and emaciated:
your body already stiffening in death.
The lashes of the centuries have fallen on your back
and you have borne it silently, like some noble Western Lady
as she waves away a sigh with with her kerchief.
Oh, you have spent the night under those low eaves
Oh, how the rain ... drips ... drips ...

1973

Untitled

All over the befuddled land,
the coarse faces of the People and their groaning hands.
Before the People, an endless expanse of hardship.
Storm lanterns sway in the wind.
The night sleeps soundly, but eyes are open wide:
You can hear the great snoring Emperor with his rotting teeth.

1973

Untitled

The blood of one class has drained away,
the archers of one class are still loosing their arrows:
that dull, indifferent sky
China's ancient dream, haunted by ghosts from the underworld,
as the coal-grey changeable moon
rises at the edge of history's desert,
in the pitch black empty city
we hear again the urgent knocking of red terror.

1974

Mansion

All sound has gradually faded away,
the night watchman is carrying a red lantern
stealthily back and forth before the window
and its light blends into the dark purple kisses
while moonlight falls in scars.

Now is the dead of night when the troubled spirit is beset by
trivialities.

Servants in the front hall long before have scrambled to their
feet.
A pair of black hands is piously winnowing the air:
Someone whispers the question, 'What!?'
startling a raven lost in sleep.

1972

IMAGES

Young Girls' Polka

The same kind of pride, same kind of trickery,
these freed girls
these girls who would be empresses
will, for love, go to the end of the earth
will follow good-for-nothings, never cease to be faithful.

1973

Boy

You created mankind, didn't create freedom,
you created woman, didn't create love.
    God, so mediocre
    God, you are so mediocre!

1973

Youth

Nothingness, from kissed lips
Slips out, bearing a strand of
Undetected consciousness:

On that street where I madly pursued women
Today, workmen wearing white gloves
Are calmly spraying insecticide ...

1973

Crows

Ashes drifting slowly
over the emptiness of a crematorium:
these black, pall-bearing angels
seem a flock of musical notes
fleeing the dusk,
as death alights amongst men ...

And the eyes which follow them off
over the mute, empty stage
of the sky
are countless, still things past,
steeped in their own tragedy,
continually crying out, without words
    or hope.

1974

Dusk

Loneliness secretly awakes,
details are also stealthily advancing.
The poet twitches, like a beetle
producing unknown feelings
as usual, in a dusk broken by hired servants.

1973

Dusk

When the risk-braving lover
with awl-shaped buttocks
probingly rises
it's as if the town also has been aroused,
is about to fiercely shake off its locks, and threatens to
open up to the woman of black night ...

1977

Night

On a night full of symbols
the moon is like a sick person's pallid face
like a mistaken, shifting time
and death, like a doctor standing before the bed:
some merciless emotions
some deeply frightening changes,
moonlight on the empty space in front of the room softly
                                                        coughs.

Moonlight, hinting clearly at exile ...

1973

Summer

Still the flowers put forth their false blooms
and the hateful trees still ceaselessly sway
and endlessly they drop their ill-omened seed.
Like a martial arts master, the sun has already scaled the wall
                                        and fled
leaving behind a youthful pupil, staring into the face of a sorry
                                        sunflower.

1975

Autumn

Left fallen on the stone steps
there are only leaves, playing cards ...
Of other things that dwell in the memory
there remains only the endless sound of the rain
the sound of the rain which now and again stopped
and came round again
like a passing warning
like a pause in a funeral oration
which then continues on ...

1975

Era

An oppressive era has revived.
The sound of a gun faintly shakes the earth.
War is stubbornly reclaiming land.
Livestock is requisitioned. Peasants return from the fields,
ploughs dripping with blood ...

1973

Liberation

The revolution goes to sleep on fists clenched tight,
'Liberation' slowly matures in his memory
like a sleepless dream, like a solitary sail
and love no longer knows where to go.
There is only God who blesses and protects his soul-stirring
   home.

1973

War

The afternoon sun lies charitably on the tombstone.
A deep low voice slowly narrates.
Tall, thin people take off army caps,
a distant life, a village full of relatives ...

1972

Sea

The sea retreats towards nightfall,
carrying off history, and carrying off sadness.
The sea is silent,
not wishing to pardon man again, nor
hear man's praise again ...

1973

IN AUTUMN

Autumn, in front of a cream-coloured Western house
an old French woman, died, slowly,
in a place far, far away from her homeland.
Children who'd run up, together, led away her faithful dog,

tied a rope round its neck, hung it from a white birch
in a place not far from the corpse of its mistress.
Slowly, it died,
a pedigree French dog.

On earth turned unfamiliar
it was these children, who'd shared out the old woman's sweets,
who, together, led away her faithful dog
and hung it from a tall white birch.

Died, together, slowly,
an old French woman, a pedigree French dog,
some children, some Chinese children
in front of a cream-coloured Western house, in autumn ...

1973

TO THE RIVAL

On the cross of freedom shoot dead the father.
Your timid hand for the first time writes down: rebel.
When again you walk from doomsday towards spring,
on the road of resurrection traversing your worn out corpse,

cherishing this excitement, that blood shall not congeal in glory.
Bending over the bronze statue of the giant I doze off to sleep,
dreaming that in the winter of truth:
from the burial ground, I silently sweep away the crows ...

1973

TO THE SUN

Giving us family, giving us maxims
you make all children ride on fathers' shoulders,
giving us light, giving us shame
you make dogs wander behind poets.

Giving us time, letting us labour
you sleep long in the black night, drowning our hopes.
Baptise us, make us believe,
under your benediction, we are born and then die.

Examine the peaceful dreamland, smiling faces,
you are God's minister.
Not having suffered man's greed, man's envy
you are emperor of the soul.

Adoring fame, you encourage us to be brave,
caressing everyone's head, you value the ordinary
You create, rise in the east,
you are unfree, like a universally circulating coin!

1973

HANDICRAFT

After Marina Tsvetaeva

I write youthful base poetry
(unchaste poetry)
writing in a long narrow room
poetry raped by poets,
street corner poetry dismissed by the cafés,
that cold
now hateless poetry of mine
(itself a story).
My poetry read by no one
is just like the history of a story.
That lost pride of mine
lost love
(that aristocratic poetry of mine),
she, is finally taken as a bride by a peasant,
she, is my wasted days.

1973

TRAVELLING WITH MARGUERITE

A

Rise up crazy, Marguerite
just as once you answered back the sun:

For you, I'm going to clean out a thousand
of the the classiest jewellers in Paris.
I'll cable you a hundred thousand
mist-moistened kisses from a Caribbean beach
if only you'll cook me some English delicacy
or fry up two great hunks of Spanish steak
and then creep into your father's study
to steal me a little Turkish tobacco.
Afterwards, we two shall flee
the rowdy marriage celebrations
and set off, together, for the Black Sea
for Hawaii, or wonderful Nice.
Together with me, your comical,
unfaithful lover,
together we'll go to the seaside,
to a nude beach,
to those coffee-coloured sands, proper to poets,
and there we'll moon about and kiss and put on
straw hats and smoke our pipes and ponder as we please.

Will you? you, my Marguerite,
set out together with me, and cross over to a warm-blooded
                                            country?

To a tropical city shaded by palms
with a harbour where golden merchantmen are anchored,
where you can see a crowd of monkeys
guzzling wine under parasols,
sailors wearing silver earrings

and fluttering long eyelashes in the moonlight,
where you will be surrounded by grasping street sellers
and their flattery
and where you can buy pitted oranges.
Marguerite, don't you see in the water
so many black women
swimming there like eels.

Come away with me
Marguerite, let's
set off towards the thousand and first night of Arabia,

towards shimmering, shadowy evenings on
the Persian Gulf,
towards pink-skinned ancients from distant lands
watering peacocks with rich red burgundy
and snake-charmers with oiled, glistening skin
playing their bamboo flutes in the serpent groves of Calcutta.
We will search until we find the moonstone of India.
We will enter a palace
a palace glittering with gold and lapis lazuli,
we shall ride on the back of an elephant,
and move off into Myth.

B

So! my noble,
my unknowing Marguerite,
come together with me now
    down to the Chinese countryside
to the impoverished, peaceful countryside
to have a little look at all our
sturdy, honest, ancient people
all our stolid, wooden, hapless peasants,
our beloved, peasants.
Do you know the peasants?
These suffering children
fearfully working out their few years
in the small dark room of superstition
while the sun and providence spread their rays.

Let's go and have a look,
heavy-hearted Marguerite
— poetess:
I want you always to remember
the painful picture
of that innocent land:
the matron with pock-marked face preparing
to celebrate thanksgiving,
scrubbing the face of the child, baking the sacred offering cakes,
silently following the rustic forms
and then breaking bread
for the tragic, holy supper
of those who labour in the fields.

1973

47

DREAMS

It is past, past away, generations are past,
    joys, sorrows
of the past, like a dust-stained, travel-weary horse and cart:
    soon, we will no longer be able to see our old home ...

In those early days, in the days when we kept our vows,
    those days we walked the streets with pride,
unconcerned, and barely acknowledged one another.
    We were unadorned, we seemed to be drunk, or ill.

Now, the elation filling the last bus
fills out the day.
        Now, the curtains, tightly drawn,
    draw out the lingering afternoon.
           Now, the postman, wearing his green uniform,
    proves his resplendent existence.

That was the time of love
    that was the time we were together.
It was a brief time
    just time enough to warm to each other.

But kisses are past, they have moved away.
    Gazing tenderly, observing me carefully,
stroking me, comforting me,
    soon, soon you will say goodbye.

The time approaches when it will be acknowledged,
    your laugh without feeling, you laugh with no trace of
                sorrow,
you laugh so lightly, hurriedly,
    at the moment of parting, you laugh so lightly, hurriedly.

The stars are obscured. There you are
        standing at the drenched tram-stop
about to withdraw your hand from mine
        and slowly, deliberately slip it into your pocket.

Fled, at last they have fled.
        Those days will never be stolen back.
Like a counterfeit coin, like gorgeous eyes:
        ringing, cheating, circulating ...

For ten beautiful Sundays
        two people created a time of
secrets, vague dreams which elude the memory,
        like some glorious dawn in the country, that will not rise
                                again.

Nothing remains,
        no love, no, nothing remains.
Fully composed, you leave. Well, go.
        You will carry off another's springtime.
                        Well, carry it off.

We are through the terrifying passage of love,
        we have paid for the crime of this fearful passion.
Wiping away the damp mists in your eyes,
        what more can you say?

The past, it is already dead,
        already dead and distant in time.
Like the sharp, clean whistling of boyhood
        recalling the simplicity and gravity of my life ...

Autumn — entering the graveyard
        where pain has been dispelled and silenced,
    in Autumn, setting out the gold lettering on my gravestone:
    To suffer, because of such happiness, such good fortune,
true sorrow has not yet been revealed, true beauty as yet
unknown ——

1973

THERE COULD BE

There could be days when huge throats gulped down the fire-
                                        water.
There could be a complete, heroic drunkenness.
There could be one afternoon,
while the clock ticks behind the curtain,
thinking through the heart's trivial business:
there could be persistent, serious embarrassment.

There could be walking alone,
sitting down on a dark green chair
and closing the eyes for a moment.
There could be a comforting sigh
recalling things past that could be called happy,
forgetting the ashes
flicked off, somewhere or other.

There could be, during the days of illness,
becoming angry, doing something disgraceful.
There could be following the old habitual pathway,
following the way back home.
There could be someone to kiss you
cleanse you, and there could also be exquisite lies
waiting for you. There could be a life like this ...

It could be so good, any time, any place.
A hand, there could be, plucking a fresh flower.
Lips, there could be, touching lips.
No more storms, and no more revolutions,
wine offered up by the People to irrigate the soil.
There could be a life like this.
It could be so good, and it will be as good as you want it to be!

1973

DUSK

Rays of greenish light trailing the sun
once more, in the tiny space of my heart, the emblems are set
                                        alight:

Hallucinations, begin to move in and out of the dark wood of
                                        thought
descend to the backs of countless stampeding beasts of the field,
are bathed in the hazy brightness of the sunset.
The golden-coloured dust of twilight
now colours every image I can see
with such profundity and richness:
It is as if a group of strangers
were slowly walking towards me
right out of the sounds they make,
as if the thorns of the sick rose,
their reds and blacks,
were secretly making to surround me
in the midst of a deep valley.

1974

DEATH OF A POET

It was the time when I died,
the same stretch of ground, the same stretch of sky,
side by side with me, all so silent.
Ah, silence, such silence,
like in a dream, moonlight noble and heartless.
Thought, has probably already ceased,
is already strengthless, acknowledging frivolous life.
Ah, silence, such tender silence.
Life softly flies away, like a breeze taking its leave ...

Ah, silence, such silence,
like in a dream, moonlight noble and heartless,
in the same dusk, in the same dawn.
No elegy to be heard, and no bells tolled.
The gate to the world of departed souls, is solemnly closed,
seeing me into the funeral train which marries me to life,
demanding I reclaim talent of days gone by.
Ah, silence, such perpetual silence,
there is no reply, and there is no echo,
there are just ghosts' torches, illuminating my whole life ...

1974

GALLERY

A

Easing out from the steam at the platform and blindly on,
although the glimmer of dawn, moment by moment, opens to
                                    brightness,
although village by-ways are lost on the clean edge of the
                                    horizon:
the black, untilled earth
    turns slowly back towards evening ...

1979

B

That stupid, barelegged, lovesick fool
fearfully pecks at twigs
with his pointed beak
    — scattered to the sky —
while gun, powder and the hunter
slowly tighten the net of dusk.

1979

C

Cloaked in dew, standing in the dawn,
she is watching over the vineyard
like some noble matron, inspecting her flowers,
with her faded beauty, with a moving sadness:
she is smiling on them ...

1973

D

Waking up as happy as a lord:
before my eyes — in a room filled with
coloured shadows and setting sunlight,
wrapped in a candy-striped bath towel, a pale white hand
        reaches upwards:
it is you, combing ...

1973

E

That beautiful throat of hers sings under the night sky
and in her basket, she gathers those stars her notes have shaken
down.
She walks into the depths of the wood, and goes on
singing into our dreams ...

1979

F

See, the window fills with reassuring sunlight
shining on my palette, on my rifle
on my single army bunk:
and now here you are
— even during the days of waiting —
    you've come.

1975

G

Darkness about to fall:
and your refusal of all but silence
is filled with pure, absolute emotion.
Your hair has caught the twilight in its web
and the deep blackness of your eyes
is blind
    to the lamplight.

1974

H

Ah well
        not only
does the night
obscure your face
it also transforms the sounds you make:
I can hear
our thoughts
moving forwards in silence
like a sleigh
gliding on
    over our wounds ...

1979

INSTRUCTION

Just in the space of a night, the wound broke open
even the books on the bookshelf forsook them.
There is only the modern magnificent singer
with a hoarse voice, singing softly,
next to an ear:
    night of a noble, night of a century.
They have already been eliminated by society's jungle
and dealt with according to this sort of theme:
they merely appeared to serve as a foil for
the world's misery.
Misery
has become their life's duty

Who says the theme of their early life was bright and cheerful?
Even now, they think that that is a pernicious saying.
In an evening with a totally artless plot
that lamplight has its source in illusion.
All they see is only, is merely
a monotonous rope that appears in the winter snow.
They can only go and play tirelessly,
struggle with elusive things, and
live together with immemorable things.
If the earliest yearnings are revived,
emptiness, is already the blemish of their whole life.

Their misfortune, comes from idealistic misfortune,
but their suffering is brought on themselves.
It is awareness that makes thought pointed
and through awareness blood is lost.
Thus, traditional reconciliation cannot be granted.
Although before their birth
the world, had existed uncleanly for ages,
they still want to find
the first culprit to discover 'truth'

and wait for the time
to destroy the world.

Given the nooses around their necks,
their only madness
is to pull them tighter.
But they are not comrades.
Their scattered destructive strength
still has not remotely seized the attention of society
and they are reduced to wrongdoers in the mind
merely because: They misused parables.

But, at the very end, they pray in the classroom of thought
and, when they see clearly their own writings, are comatose:
They haven't, haven't lived in the Lord's arranged time.
They are people who have missed life,
        stopped in a place where life is misunderstood.
Everything they have gone through, is merely a tragedy of birth.

1976

FOR THE OPTIMIST'S DAUGHTER

Oh, this scene of yours, it's so true to form:
just like you subscribing to a newspaper
looking up news of your own disappearance
—— optimist's daughter ——
please, come and influence me a little
and get an orchestra together for your flowers:

Look, you are already walking along the street in front of the
                                          wine shop
already casually throwing down change for the passers-by
and with a similar bearing ask: 'O, in the morning,
in the morning did you greet me?'
and using doting gestures
point at roadside flowers and plants, point at
that town pampered by you.
Just like you going back and forth in the room
passing me, opening the window
then casually picking up some small thing on the table.

Oh look at you, first using the tip of your foot
to shake the floor, then gesturing with your hand again
to threaten me with something.
If possible
you might also persist in smashing something,
but you will definitely want to wait until evening
to once more rifle through my papers
and then unaware suddenly feel dread.
You dread thought
but you never say so.

You live for moods.
Your reason for living
is to protect them cautiously
but you never say so.

The wine I gave you —— you watered the flowers with it,
and stuffed the handkerchief you'd wiped your lips with
into my hand, then
in a satisfied fashion walked away,
fondling everything, thinking of everything.
Without my permission you start talking to me
bragging
you could start everything all over again.
That's what you believe.
Not for a second are you quiet again
but you do not betray any haste at all.
Everything you do is specious,
there are just the flowers you fondled.
They are doomed tonight,
will never bloom again.

Oh, when you passed the green water-logged depression,
didn't you close your eyes,
didn't you make a present of a recollection.
You say you love yesterday's strange recollection.
Didn't you when looking at that house look, oh, look,
look for a very long time.
Doubtless you know
what it is you'll always remember,
you want to open up memory's grotto
just like driving out bats at dusk.
You want, in the instant when a cigarette is finished
to turn on the electric light, you want to be
    the master of recollections.

1977

THE OPTIMIST'S DAUGHTER'S REPLY

Huh, really? When you say:
  'You are tormenting me'
I'd really like to help you
but as for me, what do I count?

It's thought —— that makes you terrifying,
your eyes hollow as a dream
your hand twitching as if just amputated
your face now wild now calm
just having gone through a war.
There's just your heart —— I don't know if it's
a finished, boring
book.

But everything is very clear
letting me finally know you
still making feelings into a cause.
You are still diligently
broken-hearted,
or so you would have me believe,
but I fear it is no longer possible.
When you cannot even portray love
as more beautiful, then you no longer belong to
your description of it.
When you obstinately solicit smiles on my face
my world walks towards me.

That man who brings time
walks towards me.
I am compelled to go and greet him
then I can prove what you have said:
Love is a cancer
love is an incurable disease ...

1977

TIME OF FEELINGS

A

O, my love, let's
look once again at the world outside the window
look at the wine and tobacco shop as night draws in
the street wet with rain, the traffic and lovers,
look once again as the wind gets up, the town is
so desolate
fruitless trees, and how alone:
you can just feel: we are meant to be together
our time together
is a homely time
you can stop and write words on the window pane
never again silent, never again hesitant
and never again looking at me, just throwing your
arms around me ...

B

I'm awake, my love
when I discover
you are writing words right on my body
when I feel
your icy finger tip
then I do not open my eyes
because I know
you are deep in thought about me
on my body
you are deciding your fate
on my body
you are silently writing words ...

C

I've already forgotten
all about you
there is only your indifference that
is still as beautiful as in former days
there is only your sincere love that
still even now I
have not attained.

D

There is only sorrow
that still belongs to memory
that belongs in memory
the most important thing
there is only sorrow
it makes me
and you be together forever.

E

I sadly kiss you
bury my head in your bosom
like a child
caress you, smell your body
hope you
can give me a little faith
hope to be able to forget
this is leaving ...

H

My love, do not forget
we were once together
although everything is all in the past
although we have learnt to be apart
my love, still, do not forget
we were once together:
that is the small room we lived in
there is our past
there is you in a pure time
faithfully moving about for me
in the calm night
with deep feeling breathing for me
you sat comfortably on my knee
nestling close to my face
as I chatted on and on
lighting a cigarette
with a lover's hands you
pull off my clothes
and let the light in the little window
make my eyes smart until now.

I

Seeing you that way
understanding feelings
and again that way
warmly acquainted with their ins and outs
you incessantly
leave lipstick on my face
and slowly for me
close your eyes
you are preparing to
be kind to me
and softly remind me
not to exceed
not to exceed
your rules regarding time.

L

But what you want to present to me
is not scornful, and is not indifferent
you often take my hand
it is not teasing, it's merely caressing
you often smile at me kind-heartedly
making me grateful, making me grieve
you often fix
your eyes on me telling me:
with the most beautiful expression you merely
neglect me.

M

Ah, as usual you are telling
the lies that come before parting
as usual choose for me
a more gentle wound
for fear that your determination to leave me
still attracts me, for fear that
what has been learnt in leaving
still is love.

O

That was a time of short duration
that was a time when we loved each other
in the time when we loved each other
we found a place to part
that was the time of our parting
that was an endless time
in the time when we parted
we found a time to love each other.

P

Oh you are distressed
and kind too
but you don't want to come out with it
you just curl your hair into another style
oh, you hate me
and do not want to see me again
I, however am still brimming with gratitude:
in the midst of your curses —— we can frequently meet.

Q

Oh, look at you
sweet-talking me
but surreptitiously
forcefully gripping my waist tight
you can
lead me into darkness
but I don't flinch a bit
and don't feel ashamed
I of course know
you can be so very experienced
but your plot for me
is also so very experienced!

R

In order to recognize that this is definite
neither of us has nodded agreement
in order to believe this is real
I want also to forever bury it at the bottom of my heart
I wish, in this way to beautifully smash to pieces
with my soul in this way to chastely suffer
I wish to continuously mouth words never spoken
and obtain your uninterrupted reply ...

S

Still such painful feelings
when I think of you, I suffer so gently
so much so that when I think of you
I just feel unbearable happiness.

W

From another's view
I am able to sense that I
have become melancholy like this
like those gentle particulars
from within your disappearing voice once more
allow me to re-experience
allow me to
tell you
with all the things I have prepared to yield:

I have become ill
my love, I believe
the whole world has become ill
the whole world believes
at the moment when you finish your cigarette
you will certainly
send me a letter ...

1973 - 1979

WISHFUL THINKING IS THE MASTER OF REALITY

And we, are birds beak to beak
in time's story
with people
engaged in proving our differences for the last time:

The key is turned in the ear,
shadows have broken away from us.
The key turns incessantly.
We have degenerated into people,
we have become unrecognizable people.

1982

EATING MEAT

I really want to thank the skin covering my body: when
cooking in the frying pan
it protects my
sausage casing.

Then on my breast sprinkle a little
Garlic juice, my bed
is a dish.
Do you fear

the hair hanging out of the dish?

Like a face facing another face,
staring at you I ask you
to slice off

a very, very thin joke
keeping all its taste, and slip it into
your bread.
Sir:

Mustard makes my whole body itch!

1982

HELLO HELLO

Hello hello
I stretch out my hand to you

and shake hands with you
hello hello

you stretch out your hand to me
we shake till we're stiff

clasping humanity's discovery
hello hello

hello hello
a beautiful smile

a spring quivering
hello hello hello
hello hello hello
I shake your hand

five ice-cold bullets
their tips coated with red nail varnish

1983

NEWS COMES THAT LIBERATION
HAS BEEN BANISHED BY THE SPRING

Open your rose-coloured throat and breathe it out:
>   still it cannot be revealed,
always, always this word is buried in a deep mystery.

>   Of course, of course it is the sun,
>   this awkward, boiling flesh,
this fervent instrument which helps the voices to rise upwards
into the first clarion call of the scorching sun's mad virtuosity.

>   This first miracle of our lips pecked open by the birds.

More and more deeply involved in the tale,
each day we sow and each day reap.
We have made use of the fields and carried off their secrets,
>   their desire to be used,
>   where once, each day, we left behind a little nourishment.

>   Our intention, based on hateful formulae,
>   that moment, seeped into our hearts.
>   We were forced to change face
>   and had already become weapons in our enemy's hands.

The birds, the birds no longer wish to carry our images in their
>   beaks.

No more will there be days of commemoration amongst the
                                        memorable days.
The heart that fervently desires to praise now rhymes with the
                                        heart of cruelty.
Milk-sipping roses become war-loving roses.
        But more than this, always, always
        the bitter poison of the broadcasts
        is re-written as the first bulletin of Spring.

1982

WHEN THE BIER OF SPRING CROSSES INTO
THE SULPHUROUS LANDS OF EXILE

When the bier of Spring crosses into the sulphurous lands of
exile,
daybreak, at last shall be a drop of fresh blood fallen on
a carpet of green grasses, the skull at last shall be an ever higher
peak.
When the up-standing, prodigious lordling has been
liberated
all those fingers stretch upwards into the depths of the
sky.
Maddened serpents, all alike shall be entangled with
maddening lashes
and I shall make the evergreen phoenix-tree hear
my thrashing of the everlasting enemy in Heaven.

When sickness invades the land's desire, Death,
for dark night, hoards the incorruptible grain,
the edge of the plough once more cuts the soil, stirring
the children of memory who waken, coughing blood:
the sound of my weeping, at last is the sound of fortune
weeping.
When the river that carries the timber, carries the coffin wood
my green age at last recalls
the carved coffin-lid open wide: that cold, pale face of sadness.

When the Imperial Lord of Midwinter looks out over the
                                       valley of roses
mourning for late Autumn, the candlelight of the stars
        keeps vigil too over the passion of the years,
        so then at last the cold, tragic rainfall turns to blood
and the clamour as it seeps into the tides, seeps into the harp,
        and the wail of history. When the day of offering
        once more takes on the charm of Summer,
laying out a coffin for the months and years,
then too shall youthful Spring be laid to rest.

When my blood holds the blood of knowledge
then at last the knowledge of evil shall consume all knowledge
        and I shall make the cold-blooded Snow Queen hear
        the soul of the whirlwind's witness: if only, as of old,
the vessel of the holy saint is filled with the severed horns
        then shall I shed all my blood for the horns
and my green age at last shall be a memorial to Death. Death
        too, shall endow the faces of the dead with an immortal
                                       dignity.

1983

IN A FALLOW FIELD UP NORTH LIES A PLOUGH
WHICH GIVES ME PAIN

In a fallow field up North lies a plough which gives me pain:
When spring stumbles like a horse, a stone head
in an empty hearse
gathers the storm winds
of Death.

The steel strands of the storm bristle:
Under his hat
there is an empty space —— in the moment of death
his face was already snatched away
and now a red beard juts out
gathering up the majesty of the North, long since fallen fallow.

Spring it is that plucks at his heart like the toll of a bell,
like the cry of a child from the well's depths,
like a child cooking over a fire:
his pain —— is the pain of a colossus.

Sawing up felled timber
feels like sawing off a leg.
A thin filament of sound, more delicate than
the threads of sorrow
pierces the suddenly still lumberyard, pierces
the yard's desolate storehouse,
the loneliness of someone who sows a field
and reaches its end.

The weathered skin of the peasant woman,
faceless, but waving her hand
after the ploughman, whose back bends to the plough.
A tarnished mother with no memories,
still waving her hand —— descended, like the stone,
from long distant ancestors.

1983

LOOKING OUT FROM DEATH

Looking out from death you will always see
those whom all your life you ought not to see.
One can always be buried somewhere at one's leisure
sniff around at one's leisure, then bury oneself there
in a place that makes them hate.

They shovel dirt in your face.
You should thank them. And thank them again.
For your eyes will never again see your enemy.
Then from death will come,
when they are consumed by enmity, a scream
although you will never hear again:
Now that is the absolute scream of anguish!

1983

FEAR

Oh fear, I fear
what? I'm asking you:
—— What do you fear?
I'm just asking myself.

Judgement is a fearful
enemy.

But I have no enemy. I
fear more: If night
were a huge piece of orange peel
and the flesh of fruit were between my lips,
I fear —— this is possible.

This is possible. You —— what do you fear?
That my face is transparent, in it is you
looking at me. Looking at each other.
Flesh sprouting rapidly out of the same, shared face.

Unless blinded, wanting to look
directly —— look at each other
look in a glass of pitch black
milk. Unless blinded. Blinded.

I fear even more —— when being
sewn, by a simple nurse
in an operation
for the transplant of another's eyes
the heads of two children may be revealed.

One calls out
or both call out together
I fear both. Imagination fears both:

From the smashed window
I only have
a head with glass sticking out
and two abhorrent hands
fixed to the coffin lid
and they are yours
I don't want to think about it.

From the top half of a tree
saw off my
bottom half, and you ache.
Yell, you yell:
I no longer fear. I don't ache.
I don't ache at all. And then yell:
Yes, you no longer fear.

1983

DEAD, TEN DEAD

Another ten. Another
ten lions.

Things after death: not many,
but not a few —— happening to

leave over ten rigid
tongues. Very much like five pairs of

deformed wooden shoes.
Already rusted,

ten tails
very much like ten vet's assistants' hands

with ten ropes
slackening. Opening

twenty dreamy eyelids:
Sitting in a bath tub

ten lions, dumb
but alive. But dead

—— they're ten lions
who starved to death,

a story. Stories
come from ten

meddlesome throats
that tell stories.

1983

LANGUAGE IS MADE IN THE KITCHEN

If language is made in the kitchen
then the heart is the bedroom. They say:
if the heart is the bedroom,
wishful thinking is its master.

From wishful thinking expressed in the bird's eyes
the boy who fiddles with the mute
recognizes: commotion is just like metre
a brain incapable of dream
a lump of time's wasteland.

The boy who fiddles with the mute recognizes
but does not understand:
the contracepted seed
just cannot produce images.

Each seed is a reason,
a reason wanting
to be given voice, just like an address.

No speaking. The wild man smoking a cigarette.
No speaking, just pressing the walnut
into the tabletop. They say:

All, all talk
must cease —— when
the horses all around are quiet like that,
when they, inspect men's eyes ...

1983

WAKE UP

Outside the window the sky is clean
inside the box thoughts sparkle.

Only once in a hundred years a nod of the head,
only once in a thousand years an encounter.
The writing on the red brick wall is like an allegory,
clean lips clean language.

Quick   closely closely
bring our faces together for a moment
together for a short while like this:
clean lips clean sleep.

Withered leaves fall   scars turn purple.
In the first place it was all one memory.
We   received the only favour,
clean sleep clean sleep.

Do not call out   it will come.
Desire originally was a golden grain.
Listen to me   the only, the only thing
clean language clean language.

1983

THE WINDOW FOND OF WEEPING

Under the furthest patch of cloud
slide on the top of a glossy magnetic brick
lying idle outside the four seasons.

Lying idle, silent
like a mirror
reflecting me: forgetting.

It's a most enchanting pear
hanging, and shaking
'Come, it's yours' they say.

Early Spring; in the four seasons
tear a hole
'It's yours, it's for you, all along

the whole lot was for you.' Speaking,
speaking, spit out from the tree top
four sweet pips.

And the sun, across a basin, swimming
swimming, shoals of fish in the current
dashing against my head ...

1983

LONG LIFE

Let us go over the trembling of the heart
                in the season when bees gather their honey,
Listen to the breathing the grain and then open wide the eyes:
The pied colours on the backs of calves are chasing the sun's
                        moving shadows.
The sun! that was God's fruit
and his hand a golden basket overfilled with fruit.
— The horse closes his fortunate eyelids
in the way the fish might, having seen the beautiful face of a
                        fisherman.

Now it is just the same: This summer
a train had its legs crushed. The driver
walked out into the fields. There, watermelons
steamed in the heat. The fields were covered with metallic
                        slivers of sunlight.
A flock of hens were peddling their eggs in daylight.
Bright patches on the moon were tapped out on the typewriter
                        of the sky.
The horse removed its mask, made entirely of bone
and the sky lightened. Who knows what it was waiting for ...

All discussion ceased — emanating
from the teachings of the ancient breast and the seven
                        pitchforks,
from sleep and certain stale foodstuffs.
In the rose-coloured brain of the horse: the sea swept in by the
                        window,
the waves became backwash, the vital organs of things gave out.
Because they are incapable of shame.
Because they are incapable of shame.
The feeble flow of sap was stopped
and the old game of chess was still set out in the station.

A seed is re-planted deep in the memory, the universe
in the squint eyes of a fox-hunting man.
The memory of a blood-orange bleeding behind his forehead.
And yet he has heard their voices,
their voices setting into cement ...

1984

DAYBREAK

The moment of daybreak sows its seed,
our shared pain:
Day, why do you have to break?

Nobody taught us,
we have unteachable natural instincts.

An ice-cold bird, a bird of light
penetrates the roof
is on the point of vanishing
of being shared.
Everything
and it, will be no longer.

No one can teach us,
we don't want to learn.
Everything we don't like,
everything we disregard,
experience, comes from the heartless depths of the sea.

—— We come from there,
we are forever at the moment of daybreak.
Fear, we need to master fear:
Everything that is remembered
is sparkling,
illuminated by a time when we can no longer be together ——

1984

SICK PERSON

Three years ago the music stopped.
Freed fingers drew circles on the glass surface.
A small patch of sky
cut out by the window
talking.

But there is no longer any sound.
Words outside the window disperse.
Look at them turning into apples.
Sound slowly penetrates the fruit.
Smoke, always wants to return to its source.

Three years ago in a pit
I chopped down trees.
There were people with very beautiful, very beautiful faces
often standing before the trees.
Falling leaves, seeing people who wanted to sneer at me
approaching, covered the pit.

1984

LITTLE UNCLE

Many years ago, standing before the big goldfish pond,
staring at your own eyes,
without your body moving at all,
two hands wantonly paddled the water.
Ten, a hundred, a thousand
winds forcefully shut doors and windows.
He is counting.

That mysterious motion of his makes you so comfortable.
You cannot feel this way from the start,
your feelings afterwards are the same.
Saying nothing asking nothing answering nothing
but definitely not silent,
like a fruit squeezed dry of its juice,
thirty-three years.
A window opened up out of his balding head.
We call him little uncle.

Many years ago he wanted to laugh with me.
That face of his, unable to laugh,
covered by his hand.
Only many years later did he half-lift his hand away
as if protecting his hearing:
Little uncle, little uncle,
we call him little uncle.

Little uncle, little uncle,
our voices long ago abandoned him,
one after another.
Little uncle, is counting
one, then another little uncle.
Little uncle, count for us ...

1984

SKIES OF WINTER NIGHTS

My bed has four white rats for its feet.
I walk out into the night sky, as if into a cage
then skate out over the heavens.

So clear, so resonant,
the skies of winter nights,
more expansive, emptier than a deserted scrapyard.

Snowflakes are drunken moths
and the villages dotted here and there
are wine barrels buried in the snow.

'Who will come and clasp me round the neck?'
I can hear a horse
murmuring as it trots.

'Clip, clip', a huge pair of shears has begun to work.
From within a great cavern, the stars all begin to rise
and billowing waves are spied in the horse's eyes.

Ah, I feel so good.
As if I was running my hands all the way down
                    the smooth, glistening spine of a whale.
I am searching for the city where I live.

I am searching for my beloved,
there on the pedals of my bicycle, those two restless bananas.
Let the wood

rest in the timberyard and get on with its nightmare.
Let the new moon lying on the ash-coloured desert
get on and sharpen its sickle.

Not necessarily from the East:
I see the sun as a thread of pearls.
The sun is a necklace of pearls, rising in succession ...

1985

GREETINGS

Three hundred pine trees bow their heads towards me in
                                                greeting.
Ah, entering the clouds, entering the clouds,
the profile of the sorrowful prince,
his noble, sickly appearance.

Green sound, glittering jadeite beautiful eyes.
The noise of tear-drops rolling in the golden cup
    clearly heard, clearly heard.
    Under the hair, in the depths of the clouds
    the children who pick plums.

Ah, in the twelfth month the wood-chopping black peach
                                                empress,
    mother, mushroom's neighbours,
candle's sisters,
    concert hall of the ocean,
the sun falls.

Days when the emperor wears black,
invisible plums roll forwards,
they, are the chimes of the clock telling jellyfish the time.

1985

NORTHERN SEA

The northern sea, giant glass crashing in ice.
Loneliness, the loneliness of the sea before its beasts found land.
Earth, could you have known what taking away the sky
implied?

The night when wild tigers were shipped across the sea,
the shadow of a tiger crosses my face.
—— Oh, I'm revealing my life.

But in my life there is no excitement. No,
no excitement of men swapping blood.
If I cannot possess a memory —— stronger than the wind

I'll say: this ocean gets older all the time.
If I cannot rely on my hearing —— the thing that extinguishes
sound,
if I cannot study the sound of laughter,

that thing that awaits its return from the sea,
I'll say: things on a scale as negligible as my body
cannot excite me.

But what lies beyond the sky attracts my attention.
A stone lays an egg, the shadow of reality moves.
The seabed stands erect, the ocean races onwards day and night.

—— It's the first time, I have known happiness.
These are things I have never seen,
silk-like surface of a river whose waters are a bridge,

silk shaking the surface of a river whose waters crash about the
sky.
All phenomena of nature move me,
and odd happiness, has a strange affect on my mind.

At this moment when I possess time no more than usual
I hear oysters,
the sound of their shells opening as they love.

When those full of affection weep, I notice
the storm lifting up the four corners of the earth,
the earth pervaded by silence that follows wolves eating the last
                                                    child.

But from a large basket lifted up high
I see all people who have loved me,
tightly, tightly, tightly —— embracing each other ...

1984

VOICES OF THE NORTH

Some, which are united in their great openness, expand their
                                                    lungs,
stretch out their claws, bend backwards, lie down on their
                                                    chests.
Their breathing underlines what winter warmth remains,
but still they prefer the relentless cold ...

I, I was raised in the storm.
The storm held me close but let me breathe
so that it seemed there was a child weeping within me
and I wished to understand its weeping, to harrow myself.
Each grain of soil has opened its mouth.
Mother would not let the rivers weep,
        but I acknowledge this sound
        which can govern the governors.

Some voices, perhaps all voices
can be abused and buried in the earth.
We move about above their heads
while their powerful breath is restored beneath us.
The earth without feet or sound of footfall
begins to move with thunderous tread.
        All words
        will be drowned in its wordless voice!

1985

NORTHERN NIGHTS

The noiseless sharp cries of the bats touch the drumskin of dusk,
                                    faintly sounding,
evening sun, stately as a tiger turning a millstone,
air, air that has passed to us through the nostrils of horses,
light, light that has passed through the keyhole's eye.
        It flees with an arrow's swiftness
        every twilight has fled with such urgency.

The night is overfilled, and too little has flowed away with the
                                    waters,
which can never be still and are breaking. Breaking,
some nights begin and never end,
some rivers glisten and never clearly reveal their colours.
Some moments seem to struggle fiercely against the darkness
and some moments can only take place in darkness.
        That night when a woman stumbles upon a dead little
                                    animal
        language begins and life departs.

Snow has claimed the whole of an afternoon watched through
                                    the window,
an endless afternoon.
A clutch of fat women are relaxing in the open air.
They are always relaxing in every moment they recall.
The view is obscured by huge leaves.
Outside the window daylight broadly displays its idiocy.
        Picture a ship wrecked in the belly of a whale —
        — the heart desolate as beehives while the hail falls.

Where the pasture ends and the city begins
the crops are too weary to grow, grapes have withered from
                                        fatigue,
the stars have all gone out, are turned to bags of stones
and rays of moonlight enter the room, covering the walls with
                                        holes.
We realize and so we should:
Time is turning homewards and Life is a child leaving school.
     The world is a window and outside the window is a horse
     which has devoured a thousand lamp-lights and now is
                                        neighing:

A huge foot crosses the fields, strides over the ridgeway.
Prehistoric man raises fossils high to strike our heads.
In our minds, illumined like lamps
there is still a tract of savage forest
where deer are bleeding. On paths of snow, still gliding on,
there is a shivering of music, the trees continue to lay down
                                        their lives.
     There is a beginning, a beginning before the beginning
     there is a reunion, a reunion at the very time of reunion.

1985

MILESTONES

A main road attracts the very first direction that makes you
                                                    dizzy.
That is your starting point. Clouds envelop your head,
prepare to give you a job.
That is your starting point,
that is your starting point.
When the gaol squeezes its temperament into a city
brides and stones in the middle of the street hold you tight.
Every year's snowfall is your old jacket.
The sky, however, is always a blue university.

The sky, that miserably pale sky,
that sky whose face has just been pinched
agrees to your smiling. Your beard
is hurriedly eating.
When you pursue the big tree that cuts through time.
Golden rats crossing the water, dream of you:
You are a crinkled broad bean in a fierce storm.
You are a stool, belonging to the ocean.

Wanting you, by humanity's seaside, to study from the
                                                    beginning,
to seek yourself, on the route where you know yourself.
Northern snow is your road,
the flesh on your shoulders is your food.
The traveller who doesn't turn his head,
everything you hold in contempt, will not vanish.

1985

WALKING

Out of the slow unarrived-at reason
you go forward.
Just starting off,
just starting off
and never able to arrive.
You know, you know
and you go on
in a box turned upside down,
head facing the ground you advance on the lid of the box,
walking always walking until
you tramp to a halt.

You walk through this city in the most stupid fashion.

1985

SHRUBS

What we've said over and over they can't hear.
They see each other but cannot see.
On the surface see but cannot see.
Roots

nevertheless, seek each other in the mud
and on discovery twist one another to death.
Amongst us there are people
who call this behaviour:
love.

Lovers who have just climbed the trees
Are pondering this too.
They call it:
making love.

1985

DANCING PARTNER

A small timid animal
is whispering from your throat,
a minute sensation:
your fingertips
drawn over my back
ah, my sensation passes away
into their attention:

You seem constrained,
and call to mind some other man:
the two of you gazing at each other
while I am suddenly grown old ...

1985

DESIRE

Sit in a corner of the city
Sit here
Sit on your left foot
Sit on your little toe
Sit on the very edge of your toenail
                                        Use
your knees, glide on glass knee-caps —
I'm
        crystalline, liquid, the empty liquor of the air,
        a blue skeleton glowing through translucent flesh.
        I am — at three in the morning —
                    I am the twitching leg of a
                                        chair.

        I come closer to you in my imagination,
        size you up against your flaws,
        using my withered hand, that five-petalled rose
        completely anaesthetized,
        using my eye, the opening for a chevron-shaped
        wound: Ignorance has sucked me in.
        Two ropes intertwined
        two keys unlocking each other
        two clocks reading one another's time,
and then
        and then there are your thirty-two glistening teeth
        increasing the ignorance that has sucked me in.
        Desire has gulped down something more powerful:
        sickness is more simulating than health!
                                'But
don't
        stand in the desert rubbing your hands!'
        Your voice drifts down over the ages,
        your eyelashes sleep like the wild grasses,

your eyebrows shine like the light from clippers on
tendrils,
your fingers are a tight clutch of ten youthful bodies. You
are,
you are a violin wearing red silk around its neck.
　'You mustn't be weary!'
You are a nurse, calmly, silently nursing the sea,
you are my lover, your breathing is low but goes on...
At

the moment when the birds' flesh-coloured claws grapple:
that moment, the one moment, just at that moment
a shadow enters another shadow
and you are a mirror reflecting a thousand mirrors.
Perhaps there is you and me, perhaps there is me and
another, perhaps
there are only two young dancers
determined
to step out and uphold this world!

1986

OCTOBER SKIES

October skies drift over the idiotic faces of milking calves.
New pasture, bowing to the May soil, makes its tearful plaint.
A hand snatches up some clay to stop the horse's ears. Listen:
through the dark circles of the underworld,
                            someone is crawling forward
                                        on their nails!

Just so, the fingers of my hand become an imaginary plum tree,
my legs become a plough half-kneeling in the clay.
Following the scraping sounds of a steel shovel,
I sweat

to bury the sobbing, deep, deep underground,
and bury the power of hearing beside it:
All that we knew of the sky in our youth,
is laid out under coffin-wood.

The rarified air seduces me:
faces slowly sinking down,
others rising slowly from the old,
conflict becomes an exchange of existences!

Grey clouds roll at the horizon where sunflowers frown:
how many hands withered by lightning, how many heads
                                        cutting through the
                                        wind.
Sleep now.   Open fields.   Listen:
the sear grasslands echo with thin sound of gilded bells ...

1986

DUMB CHILD

That man's eyes stare out from your face,
stare, stare at that woman.
Clutching the wall, clutching its face,
in the time it takes to give birth to a child
your little shape
protrudes from the shell-like bedroom.
Those two flesh doors throbbing red
and your body
are saws.

Violently shaking fruit trees
the dumb child hides its head.
Stuttered lust, the odour of rose-coloured armpits
lingers under the pornographic coffin.
Silk made of flesh, jellyfish skin
pulled into a wail of silk stockings.
Dumb child shouting, shouting a whole winter's anger:
All night that man agitatedly tears paper,
all night he curses her, calls her a devil!

1986

SOLICITUDE

Early morning, the sound of talking in the bird's stomach
startles the mother awake. Before awakening (on a bloody
                                        pillow
is drawn: how fields fall asleep)
the bird, a little thumb sticking out from a branch,
singing, a song like the wind
snatching away its beak.
The bird's head,
a little golden glistening chisel.
Its beak, a shovel-shaped ray of light
turns over lava hidden in the layers of the earth
'Come, we'll plant together
            the world's solicitude!'

The bird sings with an unbroken voice
With a stubborn head it studies a kernel
(inside is wrapped eternal hunger).
In this sixteen-year-old bird's face
two terrifying black eye sockets,
inverted binoculars,
out of which hefty hunters are shot
like a crowd of swaying students
with 'eternally lonely' written on their knapsacks.

Inspecting the world through gaps between one's fingers,
                                    mother
at this very moment locks her hair in the cabinet.
A flash of ugly lightening twists her face
(like the prospect of growth-rings pondering inside a
tree trunk). Snow, shaking millions of white hands,
falling, on the snowy path.
Two lines of crooked footprints
Left behind by ten frozen, tender toes.
A dwarf like a black overcoat
is walking through filthy fields annoying them terribly.

Then suddenly, from the layers of walnuts,
from a wheat field,
I recognize my own inner mind:
a bloody, foolish torrent,
a milky embrace
I drank down this morning,
this morning I came.

1986

MOVING HOUSE

The rats of winter scatter this afternoon of thaw
and I come up with the idea of moving house.
I let the hooks hang empty
and load the pictures onto my sleigh.
The writing table, I shift out into the centre of the countryside.
I hadn't noticed that the entire horizon had long been lined with
                                                                    standing
figures,
their hands all fixed to the handles of a barrow.

What is it that they are lifting? —— the flesh of the land,
glistening like gold as it is shaken. I hadn't noticed
that all around the trees were dressed like me:
upper body wearing black,
lower body: naked trunks
inscribed: Woods for sale.

1986

REFASHIONING

Using refashioned tools, refashion language.
Using refashioned language
continue to refashion.

Every generation
paws over this table.
As for this generation

he
just stretched out a hand.
Girls started to laugh

when he realized,
he laughed with them
until he became even more laughable:

He just stretched out a hand.
The water stopped flowing.
He moved his hand.

The water didn't flow again ...

1987

CHOSEN

It is definitely in the morning.
There is absolutely nothing in the mirror; you turn round.
The keyhole to the single hotel room becomes a man's glass eye.
You let out your first scream.

The ocean, just then bores through an oyster.
Thereupon, suddenly, you discover, you have already placed
yourself in
a story forced open by time.

Solitary, but there again not faintly alone,
with unknown beliefs nourish
a boy.

The weight in your stomach
Breathes, sliced into a lump of
rigidly fixed quantity.

Some stars embrace sharp stones,
start to dance vigorously.
They are very much like the man's face

and he wants to translate them into his future image.
Thereupon, you scream again
and the sound of screaming brings a doctor.

Ears are bound with white gauze,
arms bear a medical instrument kit for trimming infants'
eyelashes.

Trees that lie low beside the road

also stand up together.
This final scream is:
'Mother's sin of youth!'

1987

LEGACY

Whisky gets drunk in the dim brain, helps me
dig open my sleep:
place myself on snow dreamt of by the blindman.
Father, I dreamt of the fountainhead of dream.

Dream, is a farmer standing firm.
Metal horse dung heaped into a road.
Superfluous black clouds growing out from one's hair.
With leaded feet stamp, stamp the weight under one's feet
—— mileage, reined in tight.
I, am led
to embrace a complete human form encapsulated in birch bark.
Father, another life is starting.

Father, that is the same life.
Hands advance fumbling, along the wall.
Dead man's feet, walking up and down in the air.
Footprints have all been built into the wall.
Beginning with the man, milk
is the start of whimpering.
Father, I hear the sound of their unblushing crying
coming from the cloud's human form greatly mourning.
        The crying sound is:
        'In what you forget, we already have aged.'

Trees are weary with mourning. Dead men
surround them. The command of the dead:
        'Continue mourning.'

1987

MY UNCLE

When from childhood I look down into the deep lavatory pit
my uncle is just exchanging glances with a bull.
In their shared gaze
I think there is an objective:
To allow all light rays in the shadow nowhere to hide!

When a hovering football pitch passed over the school,
a hint of reality-dissolving possibility,
my uncle's enlarged eyes
could see directly the empty sun frozen at the North Pole
and my uncle wants to use tweezers —— to put the sun back in
history.

Because of this I believed the sky could be moved.
My uncle often returned from there,
striding, with a planner's steps, out of his plans.
I believed even more: my uncle with the sound of an opening
door wanted
to shut himself in —— with a sort of flashback,

my uncle wanted to repair clocks,
as if beforehand he had breathed in enough premonitions.
That error he wanted to correct
has already been completed by missed time:
We have all because of this been reduced to the liberated!

Even now that cloud-enclosed tobacco smell still chokes me.
Following the direction of the disappearing tram lines,
I see a wheatfield out of which my uncle's beard is growing.
My uncle has long worn a red scarf,
all along has run away from the Earth ——

1988

STUPID GIRL

In the pitch black night dyeing mother's hair, the sound of
                                                    horseshoes
approaches. Mother's coffin
starts to put on clothing for mother.
Mother's shoes, alone climb up the tree.
The wind left for mother, like iron refuses to disperse.
Mother's end
    means winter
    from enmity disintegrated.

Winter, has already completed its oppression.
The sound of horse hooves, blossoms on the sonorous iron
                                                    plate.
On the earth rubbed bright by the snow, the wind
says the wind is cruel,
meaning a different sort of cruelty; says
things which escape towards the sky,
are paralysed in mid-air,
meaning mother's whole life;
says mother is throwing charcoal in the fire,
is throwing a child, meaning a stupid girl,
sympathizes with the ashes in the fire,
saying this is wrong, means:
'I will offend again!'

1988

11TH FEBRUARY 1988

In memory of Sylvia Plath

1

This woman who lived in an unsociable and eccentric overcoat,
a piece of cloud stuffed full of hairpins,

her heavy buttocks give the sky afterwards
the shape of a roof that's been sat on.

In a world without her there are two children,
feeding bottles hung round their necks,

bound onto a horse's back. Their father
directs a ruthless parting kick at the horse's belly:

'You cry, you scream, you cannot stop, you
should take something for it!'

2

With pupils jumping out of their sockets you ask minutely:
                                                    'That
train packed full of shaken, confused apples, was it derailed?'

The black forest is totally without expression, replacing the
                                                    wind
sombre reason pierces through,

'When you greet them with an out-of-town accent
do they nod?' The sky's expression,

a mark left by abuse,
is like hope

at a standstill. 'And I want to eat pointed things!'
Facing the back-view of the fire sitting naked alone,

an antidotary blast of French horn —— an undecayable nerve
spits her understanding into the sky.

1988

THE ROAD TO FATHERHOOD

The chair back bowed by twelve seasons of sitting, my hands
swollen by beatings, watching over wheatfields,
these strokes of winter's pen, growing out of the devastation:

Someone high above is calling out: 'Buy up all the shadows
cast by clouds over the furrowed fields!'
in severe tones. The mother of

my mother, emerges from her last words,
unrolls the heavy snow,
buries the cabin in such weather.

Inside the cabin, here is that famous pasture:
A young man, whose golden eyelashes grow inwards, kneels
and digs up my beloved: 'Never again will I allow you to die!'

Me, I kneel behind the young man
and dig up my mother: 'It's not that I cannot love again!'
My ancestors are kneeling behind me.

They and the straight young sapling which has gone to make a
                                        chair
rise up towards the cold, cruel emptiness,
uprooting the plants. Behind us

the pitiless planetary sphere
in iron sandals, seeks out every sign of new life,
and then continues to dig up —— the road to our fathers ...

1988

SEPTEMBER

In September, blindmen advance caressing waves of wheat. Tall
                                        wheat
emits a fragrance born of parables
—— the twenty-year-old sky

glides past the profile of a boy at study.
Opening the window I look out on trees standing still,
reciting their memories: in the forest is an empty space.

Petals rubbed to bits fall and scatter one after another
onto the Lord's face finding an eternal place of rest,
a gust of old wind that forces me to bow.

September clouds, turned to compost heaps,
the darkness before the storm, deals with the sky
covered by a tear-soaked handkerchief.

Mother, head bowed, cuts the grass, tailors immersed in their
                                        work.
The books I studied as evening approached
turn once more into the black heavy earth.

1988

BELL SOUND

No bell had sounded to awaken memory
but today I heard
it strike nine times
and wondered how many more times.
I heard it while coming out of the stables.
I walked a mile
and again I heard:
    'At what point in the struggle for better conditions
    will you succeed in increasing your servility?'

Just then, I began to envy the horse left behind in the stables.
Just then, the man riding me struck my face.

1988

THE GREAT TREE

Do you see this axe marked with its price?
Those dwarf trees of yours
wearing young boys' short trousers,
those voices opening out from buds
must surely have cut your heart to the quick.
        'Your wounds
        are far too neat.'

Do you hear the sound of the great tree gnawing its leaves?
You have heard and so you are afraid.
You are afraid and so you continue to wait,
to wait until the great tree's dream
has become the words you are dreaming now.
        'The great tree, the tree which consumes its own mother
        has gone to make axe handles!'

1988

NORTHERN EARTH

Always counting a pulse, watching a river fly into the distance,
always leaning on a wooden table, longing for heavy snow.
The sound of an axe and splitting the locusts out of the
firewood,
always when touching the wintered frozen soil, feet
know for certain, I belong here.
I belong here, I remember, I survey, I feed
instruments with raw meat, I firmly believe:
Here, right here, always here ——

In a country where a stone king stands erect with his back to the
sun,
in a big threshing ground, in an empty classroom during the
holidays,
In the snow before it leaves the deepest part of the sky.
Fifty bad clouds roll above the heads of cotton-pickers.
One hundred old women fly into outer space,
one thousand boys urinate over the horizon,
one hundred million stars continue being desolate
a century ——

Forbears with gloomy countenance darken rows of statues.
Stones, arranged at a distance from each other
in the pine forest, are hung black woollen overcoats.
To the heads of wheat are tied the red scarves of women
reapers.
        Seasons, seasons
with discipline that will never disappear
plant us in the road that history wants to take ——

Always in this season, winter reading,
goes slowly, the pages of the field
are no longer turned, every reader's head
falls into deep secrecy —— affected by the shock of opening up.

    Northern earth,
your desolation, lies in the holes being dug in you.
Your memory, has been dug away,
your expanse, through a lack of sorrow
dries up, you, are sorrow itself ——

Wherever you are, there will be sorrow.
From the temples of that defeated wheat field
seventy *mu* of corn, destroy your brain,
widening vegetable plots, no sound at all
more feeble than the grass. Already you can no longer hear.
You want to say to yourself, continuously pour out:
    'That is your gospel ...'

1988

DUODUO (original name: Li Shizheng, sometimes spelt Duo Duo in the West) was born in 1951 and spent most of his life in Peking, where he works on a national newspaper. He has been closely associated with the group of young, controversial 'modernist' poets who came to the fore after the liberalization of the late 1970s and his work has been singled out by the acknowledged leader of this group, Bei Dao, now the best-known contemporary Chinese poet in the West. Duoduo's is a distinctive voice, which selectively embraces a range of cosmopolitan influences: from Baudelaire, to Desnos, Thomas, Tsvetaeva and Plath.

Gregory Lee is a literary translator and scholar of modern Chinese literature. His *Dai Wangshu: the life and poetry of a Chinese modernist* will be published by the Chinese University of Hong Kong in August 1989.

John Cayley is a widely published literary translator and poet. He is a former member of the Chinese Section of the British Library, now working for a specialist publisher and bookseller.